MW00812515

robert lax

poems (1962–1997)

edited by john beer

wave books   seattle/new york

published by wave books
www.wavepoetry.com

wave books titles are distributed to the trade by
consortium book sales and distribution
phone: 800-283-3572 / san 631-760x

library of congress
cataloging-in-publication data
lax, robert.
[poems. selections]
poems (1962–1997) / robert lax ;
edited by john beer.—first edition.
pages cm
isbn 978-1-933517-80-3
(limited edition hardcover)
isbn 978-1-933517-76-6
(paperback: alk. paper)
i. beer, john. ii. title.
ps3523.a972a6 2013
813'.54—dc23
2013005976

designed and composed by quemadura
printed in the united states of america

the following poems appeared previously:
new poems: journeyman press, 1962;
republished in *new poems 1962/1985*,
coracle press/ottenhausen verlag, 1986,
ed. hans gappmayr. "problem in design,"
"three men," "japanese lesson," "the brand
new city": in *fables*, journeyman press, 1970;
republished in *fables/fabeln*, pendo verlag,
1983. [the night, the nights] (p. 82–83) was
published as *the nights, the days*, further-
more press, 1985. [what/can/be/sep/a/rat/ed]":
in *journal f/tagebuch f/kalymnos journal*,
pendo verlag, 1997, ed. john beer. *light*: in
aggie weston's #21 (winter 1984), ed. stuart
mills. *more scales*: the eschenau summer
press, 1997. *sea & sky*: in *lugano review*
1.3–4 (1965), ed. james fitzsimmons;
republished in *33 poems*, new directions,
1987, ed. thomas kellein. all other poems
are previously unpublished.

9 8 7 6 5 4 3 2 1

first edition

contents

In December of 1841, as he first began to contemplate a period of solitude by water, Henry David Thoreau wrote in his journal, "All true greatness runs as level a course, and is as unaspiring, as the plow in the furrow. It wears the homeliest dress and speaks the homeliest language." It's a formulation that echoes the Romantic aspiration to render the beauty of common life in simple, unelaborated words. At the same time, it has about it a glimmer of more mythic, even theophanic traditions: the least in the end revealed to be the greatest, the humble plowman the disguised Odysseus, Krishna the cowherd boy. Finally, what Thoreau offers is the kernel of a very particular vision of life, one that might equally deserve the title poetic or philosophical: a life that through its immersion in and attention to the homeliest experience might find itself at home everywhere and nowhere. Thoreau later distilled his thought of this uncanny form of greatness to a single command: "Simplify." And no American writer since has taken this advice to heart as deeply as the poet Robert Lax.

Born in Olean, New York, in 1915, Lax was a precocious child, writing and staging plays and encountering the elderly Thomas Edison at the Chautauqua Institution. As a young man, he combined stylish urbanity with profound spiritual questioning, as if a character in some unlikely collaboration between Noël Coward and Kierkegaard. At Columbia University in the 1930s, he took courses from Mark Van Doren and Jacques Barzun and edited the campus humor magazine along with classmates and lifelong friends Thomas Merton and Ad Reinhardt. Lax contributed astute, wise-cracking theater reviews, which at times sound like audition pieces for Harold Ross's *New Yorker*. He began placing poems at that august periodical shortly after his graduation and was eventually given a place on the editorial staff. He and Merton frequented Harlem nightclubs, making the acquaintance of Billie Holiday. While Reinhardt introduced him to New York's young painters, he occasionally attended parties at the home of his Greenwich Village neighbor E. E. Cummings, where he might encounter Columbia classmate John Berryman along with Robert Lowell.

At the same time, an episode from that period recounted in Merton's autobiographical *The Seven Storey Mountain* illustrates not only the seriousness with which Lax considered matters of faith, but also the influence that he had on his friend, soon to become the country's most voluble Trappist monk:

> Lax suddenly turned around and asked me the question:
> "What do you want to be, anyway?". . .
> "I don't know; I guess what I want is to be a good Catholic.". . .
> Lax did not accept it.
> "What you should say"—he told me—"what you should say is that you want to be a saint."
> A saint! The thought struck me as a little weird. I said:
> "How do you expect me to become a saint?"
> "By wanting to," said Lax, simply.

By the end of 1941, Merton had entered the monastery. Lax, who had applied for conscientious objector status because of his pacifist convictions, began exploring Orthodox Judaism and simultaneously working at the Harlem-based Catholic mission Friendship House. Soon thereafter he left New York to teach English at the University of North Carolina, where he ultimately proposed a doctoral dissertation in philosophy on Saint Thomas Aquinas; while the dissertation was never completed, he followed Merton into the Catholic Church in 1943.

Back in New York, Lax somewhat improbably, and briefly, became *Time* magazine's film critic; according to Lax, his interviewer told him that James Agee, then the senior critic, had looked like a hobo when interviewing, and that Lax looked like the next Agee. The increasingly peripatetic Lax then held a series of short-lived positions—writer for *Parade* magazine, screenwriter in Hollywood, visiting professor at Connecticut College—as he sought to realize his intense, if still somewhat obscure, aesthetic and spiritual ambitions for his own writing. Tagging along with his friend Leonard Robinson on a *New Yorker* assignment, Lax found unexpected inspiration when he met the renowned Cristiani circus family and was immediately drawn to the troupe's physical grace, intimate sense of community, and bohemian disregard for convention. An advance for a projected book enabled Lax to spend a season traveling through Canada with the circus; that essay gradually morphed into his first full-length poetic work, *The Circus of the Sun*, a richly textured allegory that closely observes a Cristiani performance and figures it for the ongoing creation of the world.

The Circus of the Sun was published by Emil Antonucci's Journeyman Books in 1959. Antonucci regularly contributed art to the progressive Catholic magazine *Jubilee*, where Lax served on the masthead as Roving Editor. (With sojourns in Marseille and Paris and a stint traveling with an Italian circus, Lax lived up to his title.) Founded for the purpose of making the circus poem available, Journeyman would go on to publish editions of Lax's work, handsomely illustrated with Antonucci's drawings and woodcuts, through the 1960s and '70s. In 1962, the publisher brought out Lax's second book, the iconic *New Poems*, republished here in its entirety. That same year, the poet visited Greece for the first time.

The Circus of the Sun was effusive and grandly metaphysical; the work in *New Poems* is often cryptic and relentlessly abstract. As Susan Howe perceived in an early study of Lax's work, the poems bear an inescapable relation to the work of Reinhardt, who was at that time embarked on his series of black-on-black paintings. Both Reinhardt's paintings and Lax's poems, Howe writes, are "classical and romantic, impersonal and personal, a reconciliation of opposites. . . They tell us that to search for infinity inside simplicity will be to find simplicity alive with messages." Lax recognized that he had made a breakthrough to a new form of poetic composition, one organized on the basis of the column rather than the line. In several reflective statements on his work, he cites 1962 as the date that marks his transition from wanderer in search of a vocation to "poet writing in a new style."

That revolution in poetic form coincided with his discovery of the landscape that would become his home for the second half of his life. Invited by former *Time* colleague Alexander Eliot to visit the Greek islands, Lax found a place where the then-minimal cost of living could allow him to devote his time to abstract poetry, while the intense vivacity of traditional Greek rural life resembled the spirit that had attracted him to the Cristianis. Within two years, Lax had established himself on the sponge-fishing center of Kalymnos. He would later relocate to the nearby island of Patmos, renowned as the site at which the book of Revelation was reputedly composed. With the exception of a few brief visits to the U.S. and annual trips to the European mainland, Lax remained on Patmos until he returned to Olean in 2000, where he died shortly thereafter.

The solitude that Lax found in Greece enabled him to focus his energies on exploring as fully as he desired the implications of the work he had done in *New Poems*. He compiled an immense body of work during thirty-five years on the islands, only a fraction of which has ever seen publication, and most of that in small press runs now long out of print. Lax and his admirers owe a deep debt of gratitude to those publishers that sustained his career during his lifetime: in addition to Antonucci's Journeyman, these include the Swiss house Pendo Verlag, founded by Bernhard Moosbrugger and Gladys

Weigner, which brought out elegant bilingual editions of Lax's poetry and prose, and Michael Lastnite's Furthermore Press, which printed dozens of Lax's poems during the 1980s. New Directions, along with Germany's Edition Hansjörg Mayer, published a landmark anthology edited by Thomas Kellein, *33 Poems*, in 1987, which included generous selections from *New Poems* along with the poem that may be Lax's masterwork, *Sea & Sky*. That book, however, is long out of print. Those who come across Lax's name today, perhaps through the collections published by Overlook Press, will find access to the major works of his career, with the exception of *The Circus of the Sun*, arduous and expensive.

The primary goal of the present collection is to remedy this, making widely available to a new generation of writers and readers some of Lax's central accomplishments. Back in 1978, Richard Kostelanetz described Robert Lax as the last unacknowledged poet of his generation. While that characterization unfairly belies the reputation that Lax has always enjoyed in certain corners of the avant-garde, especially among those attuned to visual and concrete poetry, all the same a larger recognition of the singularity and scope of Lax's poetic achievement is long overdue.

One obstacle to that recognition, which immediately confronts any editor hoping to compile a volume like this one, is the variety of Lax's literary production. His writings encompass compressed humorous sketches (*Episodes*), abstract poems restricted to color words (*Black & White*), extended prose journals, and spiritual meditations (*21 Pages*), just to name a few of his favored genres. At the same time, statements in interviews and Lax's own writing practice leave little question that he continued throughout his life to conceive of himself primarily as a poet, and to see the composition and publication of *New Poems* as a definitive moment in his poetic development. My initial editorial instinct, from the moment that Wave proposed this project, was that a reprinting of the whole of *New Poems* would have a central place.

That the book has been so long unavailable—after its initial publication, the only full reprinting has been in a 1986 British/German edition—should be quite as remarkable as it would be were *For Love* or *After Lorca* or Berrigan's *Sonnets* known only to a handful of aficionados and rare-book collectors. Like these others, Lax's slim volume discovers a new realm of expressive possibility. Many of the tensions playfully explored throughout the poems spring up in the first few stanzas of the reticent opening piece:

> one stone
> one stone
> one stone
>
> i lift
> one stone
> one stone
>
> i lift
> one stone
> and i am
> thinking

At once the visual rhyme and sonic disjunction of *one* and *stone* belie the simplicity in which the language seeks to record the most unremarkable of items. And the gesture with which the attention singles out that one stone from possible others is also called into question with the stanza's repetition, splitting the one rock into three at the same time that it subordinates the unity of the line *one stone* to the pull of vertical movement. The second stanza matches the basic quiddity of the stone with the basic action of lifting, though complicated by the movement of the reader's eye, which is not rising but descending. The third stanza brings the final piece into play with the Cartesian assertion, "and i am/thinking." This last move opens the possibility that any given moment in the poem depicts not an actual object or action but the thought of that object or action, even as the meditative repetition of the poem aims to erase that distinction: to make the thought and the object exactly correspond.

While such reflections may establish the intellectual interest of this unassuming writing, all the more noteworthy is the poetry's profound expressive capability. As a reader, I find the successive iterations of these stanzas taking on aspects by turns calm, anxious, isolated, reassured, and ultimately open to the ongoing potential for these and other affective states. As one reads more deeply into the poetry, whether in *New Poems* or the other work that flows from it, one almost inevitably wrestles with the issue of how much of this emotional and spiritual significance inheres in the work itself and how much is projected by the reader into the experience of the poem. It may be that Lax's poetry, like Reinhardt's black paintings, are intended to provoke just such a dialogue, to invite a participation that might at times come to seem a confrontation, and then a self-confrontation, until one ends up back before the work again, but with the sense that both the self and the work have been changed through the process.

In such a manner, the work gathered here might seem closely aligned with the aspect of Thoreau's and Emerson's writing which the philosopher Stanley Cavell has characterized as perfectionist, a dynamic according to which the reader finds herself being read by the text as much as she reads it. Any proper reading of such a work demands a participation that will reveal the reader's mind and life to herself. Lax's work may also share some of the qualities that Merton describes in the monastic tradition of contemplative prayer, though perhaps in less violent terms than Merton portrays it:

> The monk confronts his own humanity and that of his world at the deepest and most central point where the void seems to open out into black despair. The monk confronts this serious possibility, and rejects it. . . The option of

absolute despair is turned into perfect hope by the pure and humble supplication of monastic prayer. The monk faces the worst, and discovers in it the hope of the best.

Some sign of the desperation that Merton invokes is visible in the threat of meaninglessness that Lax's repetitions stir up in the language's most fundamental words: *is*, *say*, or *never*. But overemphasizing this element would obscure what seems to me the signal quality of Lax's writing: its assurance, less in its own abilities than in the potential for the simplest words and most common experiences to speak across our human separateness. The poems may dance on the edge of meaninglessness's abyss, but they never plunge within.

New Poems found its most welcoming audience among the practitioners and admirers of concrete poetry, the movement initiated by Swiss poet Eugen Gomringer and Brazilian brothers Augusto and Haroldo de Campos which sought to place the visual dimension of words and letterforms on an equal footing with sound and sense in poetry. Ian Hamilton Finlay placed a Lax poem on the cover of the "concrete number" of his British journal *Poor. Old. Tired. Horse.*; his poems were included in the seminal anthology *Concrete Poetry: A World View*; Lax corresponded with Fluxus concrete poet Emmett Williams and the young innovator Aram Saroyan; he regularly visited the annual Bielefeld conference of concrete and sound poets. All the same, as acknowledged in discussions of Lax's writing by the pioneering scholars of concrete poetry Mary Ellen Solt and Stephen Bann, Lax's work always sat somewhat uneasily alongside the work of Gomringer, the de Camposes, or Finlay. Where concrete poetry emphasized the material conditions of writing, Lax's poetry sought insistently to transcend those conditions. And while the visual impact of Lax's narrow columns of words and syllables is undeniable, the primary impetus behind Lax's vertical structure is not visual but musical: both in its regulation of the repetitive patterns of sound that create the poetry's deeply meditative effect, and in its tightening of the

aperture of the reader's attention, inviting intense concentration on individ-
ual words and syllables.

Likewise, the frequent characterization of Lax as a "minimalist" poet,
on the model of the visual art of Donald Judd or the music of Philip Glass,
invites misunderstanding of the work. To be sure, just as "concrete" ges-
tures toward the centrality of the individual word or syllable in Lax's writ-
ing, "minimal" notes correctly that these are poems that generate their
effects out of the smallest units of semantic significance. But both labels
tend to figure Lax's work as more oppositional and consciously avant-garde
than it really is, and thereby obscure the deeper continuities between Lax
and the lyric tradition. No doubt it is possible to read these poems as partic-
ularly astringent moves in a formal game. Unless one also registers how the
poems respond at a fundamental level to the wonder and pathos of existence,
appreciates that they are saturated with referentiality even as they approach
bare marks on a page, the experience of the poems will remain inert, as if
they were museum pieces rather than dynamically unfolding inquiries.

Nowhere are the maximal intentions of Lax's poetry more evident than in
the hundred and thirty pages of *Sea & Sky*. Composed in the initial years of
his time in Greece, this cameo epic fuses the techniques introduced in *New
Poems* with an expansive vision seemingly derived from the elemental land-
and seascapes that now surrounded the poet. At moments, the poem's layers
of biblical allusion, depth psychology, and natural description might seem
disorienting; through its repetitions, *Sea & Sky* works to dismantle the
boundaries between time and timelessness, flooding the reader with a mystic
apprehension of unity. And at the same time, what the poem invokes as
"a/cer/tain//rhythm," bound up with "a/cer/tain//know/ing," enables the
steady ongoing development of the piece itself to function as a stabilizing
beacon. The primacy of musical effect in Lax's writing is visible here espe-
cially in the minute adjustments of spacing for evocative effect: notice, for
instance, how the slight additional spacing in the repetitions of

gave

him

heart

gave

him

heart

for

what

fol-

low-

'd

introduces a perceptible note of uncertainty followed by emphatic confir-
mation. In both of the quotations from the poem cited here, one can also see
the ubiquitous self-reference of the poem as well; the titular sea with its slow
movements and strong, cold currents is undoubtedly the Aegean, but it is
equally undoubtedly *Sea & Sky* itself, and the language that it so subtly
shapes. The poem works both as a highly reflexive modernist construction
and as an act of contemplative ascesis, a combination characteristic of a
poet formed by his deep admiration of both James Joyce and Saint John
of the Cross.

If *New Poems* clearly stood as the natural commencement of this book,
the signal achievement of *Sea & Sky* seemed just as naturally its conclusion.
Between them, I have eschewed chronological order, in large part because
a conventional narrative of development appears antithetical to the nature
and aspirations of Lax's work from the 1960s on. The vertical poems in
particular might best be viewed as a continual elaboration of the original

impulse to express the largest insight in the simplest language. Poems written in 1985, then, might be indistinguishable in structure, imagery, or even vocabulary from one written in 1972. That's not to say, as some of his incidental comments may have at times suggested, that Lax was careless or indifferent to distinctions of quality among his poems. His longtime process was to fill up notebooks with several handwritten poems per day and then occasionally retype the poems, noting those he thought worthy of preservation. (Perhaps unsurprisingly, these were generally the ones in the most straightforward form or language.) In similar spirit, this collection seeks to pick out from his vast body of work, published and unpublished, some of the most striking and evocative pieces.

These range from the careful, almost haiku observations of *Nights & Days* through the austerely sublime *Light* to the quirky oppositions of *More Scales*. The longer selections are counterpointed with individual poems, several from the 1970 collection *Fables*. These arch and mysterious little narratives may seem altogether prolix against the backdrop of the more reticent and meditative poems surrounding them, but one can locate a predecessor for them in the oblique episode found in *New Poems* that begins: "'are you a visitor?' asked/the dog." Most of the other single poems come from typescripts composed in the early '70s. They're included in part to illustrate Lax's remarkable ability to compose with a few brushstrokes as well as on the mammoth scale of *Sea & Sky*.

It's my hope that this collection can introduce readers to the variety and depth of Robert Lax's works, and not only because of their status as brilliant and unjustly neglected aesthetic pieces, but also for their more inchoate aspirations. Although Lax might have balked at so direct a statement, his poems and journals throughout his life reflect a conviction that we have the kind of civilization we do, with our thoughtless brutalities to one another and to nature, because we've fallen a little too much out of love with the world. These poems attempt to enact a reconciliation, "sketchings of that ideal place toward which all hopes aspire," as he once put it. A poem from the 1995 volume *Notes/Notizen* not included in the body of this collection reads:

turn
ing

the
jun
gle

in
to

a

gar
den

with
out

des
troy
ing

a
sin
gle

flow
er

Here is the jungle; here is the garden.   —John Beer

new poems

1962

one stone
one stone
one stone

i lift
one stone
one stone

i lift
one stone
and i am
thinking

i am
thinking
as i lift
one stone

one stone
one stone
one stone

i lift
one stone
one stone

i lift
one stone
and i am
thinking

i am
thinking
as i lift
one stone

i am
thinking
as i lift
one stone
one stone

i am
thinking
as i lift
one stone

one stone
one stone
one stone

i lift
one stone
one stone

i lift
one stone
and i am
thinking

darkness
oh the darkness
oh the darkness
of the wood

no light
no light at all
comes through
the trees

when will the light
come stealing,
when will the light
come stealing,
when will the light
come stealing
through the forest?

darkness
oh the darkness
of the wood

no light
no light at all
comes through
the trees.

andalusian proverb

rooster
rooster
rooster

rooster
with your
head cut
off:

what
are you
thinking
now,

you rooster,
what are you
thinking now
of the bloody
morning?

the air
and the dream;

the dream
and the air:

the flow
of the dream;

the flow
of the air.

The Maximum Capacity
of this room
is 262 people
262 people
The Maximum Capacity
of this room
is 262 people

word
word
word

a word
a word
a word

one word
two words
one word
two words

a word
a word
a word

forms
forms
forms

basic
basic
forms

basic
basic
basic
basic
basic
basic
forms

push
pull
push
pull
push
pull
push
pull
push

the first goodbye

the second goodbye

the third goodbye

the fourth goodbye

the fifth goodbye

the sixth goodbye

the seventh goodbye

the eighth goodbye

the ninth goodbye

the tenth goodbye

the eleventh goodbye

the twelfth goodbye

the hundred & twenty-first goodbye

the hundred & forty-fourth goodbye

the hundred & eighty-ninth goodbye

goodbye

goodbye

goodbye

is
is
is
is
is
is
is

is
is
is
is
is
is
is

is
is
is

is
is
is

is
is
is
is
is
is
is

even a lie
is a psychic
fact

even a lie
is a psychic
fact

my uncle told
a lie to my aunt;
my aunt believed
him and married
my uncle

even a lie
is a psychic
fact
a lie is a
psychic fact

my aunt had children
and told them lies;
the children believed
them
and grew up strong

even a lie
is a psychic
fact
a lie is a psychic
fact

the children lied
to their future
wives;
the wives believed
them
and married them
young

(and now the whole
family is flat
on its back)

even a lie
is a psychic fact;
a lie is a psychic
fact.

1 2 3
1 2 3
1 2 3 4
1 2 3

1 2 3
1 2 3
1 2 3 4
1 2 3

1 2 3 4
1 2 3 4
1 2 3 4
1 2 3

1 2 3
1 2 3
1 2 3 4
1 2 3

A A A
A A A
A A A A
A A A

A A A
A A A
A A A A
A A A

A A A A
A A A A
A A A A
A A A

A A A
A A A
A A A A
A A A

fire
water
earth
& air

fire
water
earth
& air

fire
water
earth
& air

fire
water
earth
& air

sky
& sky
& sky
& sky

sky
& sky
& sky
& sky

fire
water
earth
& air

fire
water
earth
& air

fire
water
earth
& air

fire
water
earth
& air

sky
& sky
& sky
& sky

sky
& sky
& sky
& sky

sky
& sky
& sky
& sky

sky
& sky
& sky
& sky

summer
autumn
winter
spring

summer
autumn
winter
spring

summer
autumn
winter
spring

summer
autumn
winter
spring

sky
& sky
& sky
& sky

sky
& sky
& sky
& sky

sky
& sky
& sky
& sky

sky
& sky
& sky
& sky

fire
water
earth
& air

fire
water
earth
& air

fire
water
earth
& air

fire
water
earth
& air

summer
autumn
winter
spring

summer
autumn
winter
spring

summer
autumn
winter
spring

summer
autumn
winter
spring

fire
water
earth
& air

fire
water
earth
& air

fire
water
earth
& air

fire
water
earth
& air

sky
& sky
& sky
& sky

one bird
two birds

one bird
two birds

two birds
one bird

two birds
one bird

one bird
two birds

one bird
two birds

two birds
one bird

two birds
one bird

one

love &
death

are blood
& bone

love &
death

are bread
& stone

love &
death
are rose
& thorn

(love &
death

are sheep
& shorn)

in the dark
in the dark
my love
is lying
in the
park

my love
is lying
in the park
and listening
to the stream

. . . .
. . . .
. . . .
. . . .

in the dark
in the dark
my love
is lying
in the park

my love
is lying
in the park
and listening
to the stream

no

no

no

yes

yes

yes

no

no

no

yes

yes

yes

no

no

no

yes

yes

yes

yes

yes

yes

no

no

no

yes

yes

yes

no

no

no

never

never

never

never

never

never

never

never

never

never

never

never

what does it
matter if
i am an
insomniac?

if the machine,
my brain
doesn't work?

if the plant,
my brain,
is over-
active?

if the animal,
my brain,
is wild?

what does it
matter if
after some time
in the light,
in the night
i die?

what if my
poems,
neatly rolled
in a jar,

are read
are not read?

do keep
do not keep

someone else
awake all
night
sometime?

"are you a visitor?" asked
the dog.

"yes," i answered.

"only a visitor?" asked
the dog.

"yes," i answered.

"take me with you," said
the dog.

never a root
without a tree
never a tree
without a bird
never a bird
without a song
never a song
without a sky

never a sky
without a song
never a song
without a bird
never a bird
without a tree
never a tree
without a root

never a root
without a tree

in me
in me
in me

is the
watcher

in me
in me
in me

is the
watcher

in me
is the
watcher

in me
is the
watcher

in me
in me
in me

is the
watcher

Theo,
Theo,

you don't
hate me

even if
you are
dead,
do you?

you don't
hate me

you don't
hate me

even if
you are
dead

à cause
de ma folie

you don't

hate me

you don't
hate me

you don't
hate me,

Theo,

do you?

you don't hate
me

you don't hate
me

you don't hate
me

Theo, do you?

you don't hate
me

you don't hate
me

you don't hate
me

Theo, do you?

even if
you are
dead

à cause
de ma folie,

you don't hate
me

you don't hate
me

you don't hate
me,

Theo, do you?

you don't
hate me

you don't
hate me

you don't
hate me

you don't
hate me

Theo,
do you?

even if
you are
dead

à cause
de ma folie

even if
you are
dead

à cause
de ma
folie

you don't
hate me

you don't
hate me

you don't
hate me

Theo,
do you?

you don't
hate me

you don't
hate me

you don't
hate me,

Theo,
do you?

into the heart
of the city,
the city

into the heart
of the city

the pike
was digging

the pike
was digging

into the heart
of the city

the first
thing to do
is admit
your defeat

the first
is admit
your defeat

the first
thing to do
is admit
your defeat
the first
is admit
your defeat

the next
thing to do

is to start
in again

the next
is to start
in again

the next
thing to do

is to start
in again

the next
is to start
in again

i do
not wish

to touch
thee, no:

i wish
to flow
within
thy veins

i wish
to flow
within
thy veins

i wish
to flow
within
thy veins

he was
following
a hero

following
a hero

following
a hero

he had
never

seen

hurry
up
hurry
up
hurry
up

slow
down
slow
down
slow
down

hurry
up
slow
down

hurry
up
slow
down

hurry
up
hurry
up

slow
down

every
night
in the
world

is a
night

in the
hospital

things
into
words

words
into
things

things
into
words

words
into
things

words
into
things

words
into
things

things
into
words

words
into
things

all of us
in the
darkened
half

breathe
in
breathe
out

like
boatmen
rowing

you will dissolve
before me
you will dissolve
before me
you will dissolve
before me
i shall not watch
you go

you will dissolve
before me
you will dissolve
before me
you will dissolve
before me

i shall not watch
you go

i shall not watch
you go

you will dissolve
before me
you will dissolve
before me

you will dissolve
before me

but i shall not watch
you go

my son
my son

all my
life

all my
life

i've been
wanting
to tell
you

i've been
wanting
to tell
you

this

this

this

this

this

life
life

life
life
life

life
life

life
life
life

life
life
life

life
life
life

life
life

life
life
life

death
death
death

death
death
death

death
death

death
death

death
death
death

i am
thinking
as i lift
one stone:

one stone
one stone
one stone

one stone
one stone
one stone

one stone
one stone

one stone
one stone

one stone
one stone
one stone

two fables

problem in design

what if you like to draw
big flowers

but what if some sage has told
you that there is
nothing more
beautiful

nothing more
beautiful

nothing more
beautiful

than a
straight
line

what should
you draw:
big
flow
ers
?
straight
lines
?

i think
you should
draw

big
flow
ers

big
flow
ers

big
flow
ers

big
flow
ers

big
flow
ers

big
flow
ers

big
flow
ers

big
flow
ers

un
til

they
be
come

a
straight

line

[1970]

three men

three men
found a
treasure

under a
tree

well,
we're a
lucky three-
some, said
the first man

you two guys
are the lucky
ones, said
the second

i don't suppose
there's anything
there for me

oh no, said
the third—
we'll divide
it three ways

they sat
down under
the tree

& the first man
counted out

an equal
number of
pieces of
gold

for each

then they
shouldered
their packs

well, said
the first,
i think i'll
go north

i may as well
go south,
said the second

& i'll go
east, said
the third

& they went
on their ways

the first
man came to
a city

& spent
all his gold

on dancing
girls

the third
went east

& built a
great temple

the second,
however,
went south

& was
cozened out
of his pile

by farmers

the lucky
three,

said a
bird

in the
tree

lucky
three

the lucky
three

[1970]

nights & days

1981

at	black
night	giant
a	squats
dark	in
sun	the
	sea
shines	
on	his
the	arms
sea	out
	stretched
&	&
	quiets
calms	
it	the
	waves

moon
& cloud

the   his
dark   pale
a   gold
rab   en
           wife
a
cro   stands
bat   near
           him
stands
on   &
his   ap
hands   plauds

herds
of
dark
crea
tures

gath
er
in
the
sky

moon
lights
their
manes

roos
ter's
cry

cuts
the
air

shad
ow
of
night

heals
it

old   old

roos   roos

ter   ter

crows   crows

old   old

roos   roos

ter   ter

crows   crows

then   then

sev   sev

eral   eral

young   young

then   then

sev   sev

er   er

al   al

young   young

win
ter

wind

the
cock
crow

quav
ers

fal
ters

through
win
ter
air

black
bird

to
ward

foot
hold

with
news
from
the
sky

to
my
roof
top

all
in
a
tor
rent

falls
the
rain

fine
rain
fall
ing

earl
y
morn
ing

life
to
tree

peace
to
sea

the

nights

the

nights

the

days

the

days

the

earl

y

dawns

the

eve

ning

glows

the

nights

the
nights

the
days

the
days

the
dawns

the
eve
ning
glow

-

on   on   on   rocks
ly   ly   ly
make   make   make   to
                        stand
                        un
goats goats rocks der

on   to   on   the
ly   run   ly   goats
make   a   make
           bout
           the
rocks   goats
           rocks

hordes   clouds   shad
like   in   ows
camel   search
herds   of   search
          noth   ing
          ing

drift   for
over   no
hills   where
               a
               cave

as
dry
as
desert

cloud	bird	sea	cloud
o	o	un	o
ver	ver	der	ver
hill	sea	bird	hill

hill	sea	hill	bird
un	un	un	o
der	der	der	ver
cloud	bird	cloud	sea

black	green
bird	hill
black	green
bird	hill
white	white
sea	sun
white	white
sea	sun
black	black
bird	bird
black	green
bird	hill
white	white
sea	sea

whips   bird

a   shad
cross

              ow
the
walk

&

up

the

wall

he	he	he	he
he	he	he	he
is	she	is	she
part		part	
	she		she
of		of	
the		the	
sea		hills	
	part		
	of		part
	the		of
	sea		the
			hills
she		she	
	part		
she	of	she	
	the		part
	sea		of
is		is	the
part		part	sea
of		of	
the		the	
sea		hills	

sea   cool
in   in
his   his
veins   veins

green   sea
in   in
his   his
veins   veins

green   cool
sea   green
weed   weed

in   in
the   the
cool   sea

of   of
his   his
veins   veins

hill	cloud
talk	talk
hill	cloud
talk	talk
sky	sea
talk	talk
sky	sea
talk	talk
hill	hill
talk	talk
hill	hill
talk	talk
sky	sky
talk	
sky	
talk	

shad	earth	shad	shad
ow		ow	ow
	earth		
shad		on	in
ow		stone	void
	earth		
shad		stone	stone
ow	in		
	space		
		on	in
on		earth	void
stone			
	space		
		earth	
	space		earth
stone			
	space	in	
stone		space	earth
	in		
stone	void		earth
		space	
			in
on		in	void
earth		void	

i   earth
can't   gets
see   in
you   my
                  way

be
cause
of   &
this   so
light   does
                  the
                  sky

i   all
can't   your
see   cre
you   a
                  tion

                  blinds
be   me
cause
of
these
walks

two poems

what
can
be
sep
a
rat
ed
from
us

what
can
be
sep
a
rat
ed
from
us

what
can
be
sep
a
rat
ed
from
us

is
not
the
way

what
can
be
sep
a
rat
ed
from
us

what
can
be
sep
a
rat
ed
from
us

what
can
be
sep
a
rat
ed
from
us

is
not
the
way

the
way
can
not
be
sep
a
rate

the
way
can
not
be
sep
a
rate

the
way
can
not
be
sep
a
rat
ed
from
us

what	what	what	is
can	can	can	not
be	be	be	the
sep	sep	sep	way
a	a	a	
rat	rat	rat	
ed	ed	ed	-
from	from	from	
us	us	us	

[1976]

one
star

for
each
po
em

    one
    po
one   em
po
em   one
    star
for
each
star

one
star

one
star

[1973]

light

1984

light	dark
be	be
gets	gets
light	dark
light	light
be	be
gets	gets
light	dark
dark	dark
be	be
gets	gets
dark	light

light   be
               gets

be
gets   light

light

be
gets

light

dark	light
out	out
of	of
dark	light
light	dark
out	out
of	of
light	dark
light	dark
out	out
of	of
dark	light
dark	light
out	out
of	of
light	dark

dark	dark
of	in
light	to
	dark
light	light
of	in
dark	to
	light
light	light
of	in
light	to
	dark
dark	dark
of	in
dark	to
	light

light	dark
is	is
light	light
light	dark
is	is
light	light
dark	light
is	is
dark	light
dark	light
is	is
dark	light
light	light
is	is
dark	light
light	light
is	is
dark	light

○

light	dark
in	in
light	dark
light	dark
in	in
dark	dark
light	light
in	in
light	light
dark	light
in	in
dark	light
dark	light
in	in
light	dark
dark	dark
in	in
light	light
light	light
in	in
dark	light

dark	light
in	in
dark	light
dark	light
in	in
light	light
dark	dark
in	in
dark	dark
light	dark
in	in
light	dark
light	dark
in	in
dark	light
light	light
in	in
dark	dark
dark	dark
in	in
light	dark

light	dark
light	dark
light	dark
light	dark
dark	light
dark	light
dark	light
dark	light
light	dark
light	dark
light	dark
light	dark
dark	light
dark	light

light   light
in   in
dark   light

dark   dark
in   in
light   dark

light   light
in   in
dark   light

dark
in
light

○

light	light	light
light	light	light
light	light	light
light	light	light
light	light	light
light	light	
light	light	

light	light	light
light	light	light
light	light	light
light	light	light
light	light	light
light	light	
light	light	

light	light	light
light	light	light
light	light	light
light	light	light
light	light	light
light		light
light		light

light	light	light
light	light	light
light	light	light
light	light	light
light	light	light
light		light
light		light

○

ex	ex
plo	plo
sion	sion
of	of
light	light
ex	ex
plo	plo
sion	sion
of	of
light	light
ex	ex
plo	plo
sion	sion
of	of
dark	dark
ex	ex
plo	plo
sion	sion
of	of
dark	dark

ex   ex

plo   plo

sion   sion

of   of

dark   dark

ex   ex

plo   plo

sion   sion

of   of

dark   dark

ex   ex

plo   plo

sion   sion

of   of

light   light

im
plo
sions

of
dark

im
plo
sions

of
dark

im
plo
sion

of
light

im
plo
sion

of
light

im
plo
sions

of
dark

im
plo
sions

of
dark

im
plo
sion

of
light

ex	ex
plo	plo
sion	sion
of	of
light	dark
ex	ex
plo	plo
sion	sion
of	of
light	dark
ex	ex
plo	plo
sion	sion
of	of
dark	light
ex	
plo	
sion	
of	
dark	

○

cir	lad
cle	ders
of	of
light	light
cir	lad
cle	ders
of	of
light	light
cir	lad
cle	ders
of	of
dark	dark
cir	lad
cle	ders
of	of
dark	dark
cir	lad
cle	der
of	of
dark	dark

cir	lad
cle	der
of	of
dark	dark
cir	cir
cle	cle
of	of
light	light
lad	cir
ders	cle
of	of
dark	light
lad	cir
ders	cle
of	of
dark	light
lad	cir
ders	cle
of	of
light	dark

lad   cir
ders   cle

of   of
light   dark

lad   lad
ders   der

of   of
dark   dark

lad   lad
ders   der

of   of
dark   light

cir
cle

of
light

cir
cle

of
light

○

cir   cir
cle   cle

of   of
light   light

○

three poems

the giant
returns
the giant
retreats

the giant
returns
the giant
retreats

the giant
walks

the giant
sleeps

the giant
returns

the giant
retreats

[1973]

fire	fire
fire	fire
yell	yell
'd	'd
the	the
child	child
wa	wa
ter	ter
wa	wa
ter	ter
yell	yell
'd	'd
her	the
broth	oth
er	er

[1973]

now   now
i   i
will   will
send   send
them   them

now   now
i   i
will   will
send   send
them   them

now   now
i   i
will   will
send   send
them   them

the   the
rain   rain

the   the
rain   rain

now   the   now
the   rain   the
light   thun
ning   the   der
               rain

now
the
thun   now
der   now   the
        the   rain
now   light
the   ning   the
light   rain
ning   now
        the   the
now   thun   rain
the   der
thun
der

        now
now   the
the   light
rain   ning

[1973]

jacob & the angel

1981

jac	jac	an
ob	ob	gel
said	lift	lift
	ed	ed

an	jac	an
gel	ob	gel
said	lift	lift
	ed	ed

jac		
ob	jac	
said	ob	an
	fell	gel
		fell

an		
gel	jac	
said	ob	an
	fell	gel
		fell

```
jac             jac             an
ob              ob              gel
said            lift            lift
                ed              ed



an
gel
said            jac             an
                ob              gel
                lift            lift
                ed              ed



jac
ob
said            jac             an
                ob              gel
                lift            lift
                ed              ed
an
gel
said



                jac             an
                ob              gel
                lift            lift
                ed              ed
```

jac	jac	jac
ob	ob	ob
fell	said	said

	jac	jac
jac	ob	ob
ob	said	said
fell		

an		
gel	an	an
fell	gel	gel
	said	said

an	an	an
gel	gel	gel
fell	said	said

two poems

i
still
like
the
way

i
still
like
the
way

old
wan
da
lan
dow
ska

wan
da
lan
dow
ska

i
still
like
the
way

i
still
like
the
way

old
wan
da
lan
dow
ska

wan
da
lan
dow
ska

wan   hits
da   that
lan   harp
dow   si
ska   chord

hits   hits
that   that
harp   harp
si   si
chord   chord

hits
that
harp
si
chord

[1973]

ro

ber

to

ro

ber

to

ro

ber

to

cries

the

roos

ter

roos

ter

roos

ter

roos

ter

cries
my
soul

ro
ber
to

ro
ber
to

roos
ter

roos
ter

ro
ber
to

ro
ber
to

as
the
long
day

wanes

[1973]

more scales

1997

wind	si	more	more
	lence	wind	si
			lence
&		than	
si	&	si	than
lence	wind	lence	wind

the	the	more	more
one	man	one	man
	y		y
the		than	
man	the	man	than
y	one	y	one

joy	danc	more	more
	ing	joy	danc
			ing
&		than	
danc	&	danc	than
ing	joy	ing	joy

words	let	more	more
	ters	words	let
			ters
&		than	
let	&	let	than
ters	words	ters	words

calm	gen	more	more
	tle	calm	gen
			tle
&		than	
gen	&	gen	than
tle	calm	tle	calm

the	the	more	more
air	light	air	light
the	the	than	than
light	air	light	air

flow	pause	more flow	more pause
& pause	& flow	than pause	than flow

get	ly	more	more
ting	ing	get	ly
up	down	ting	ing
		up	down
&	&	than	than
ly	get	ly	up
ing	ting	ing	
down	up	down	

wig	ig	more	more
wam	loo	wig	ig
			loo
&		than	
ig	&	ig	than
loo	wig	loo	wig

swing	smooth	more swing	more smooth
& smooth	& swing	than smooth	than swing

gi	mon	more	more
ant	ster	gi	mon
		ant	ster
&	&	than	than
mon	gi	mon	gi
ster	ant	ster	ant

squares	cir	more	more
	cles	squares	cir
			cles
&		than	
cir	&	cir	than
cles	squares	cles	squares

you	me	more	more
		you	me
&	&	than	than
me	you	me	you

a	a	more	more
wake	sleep	wake	sleep
a	a	than	than
sleep	wake	sleep	wake

the	the	more	more
breeze	trees	breeze	trees

the	the	than	than
trees	breeze	trees	breeze

two fables

japanese lesson

a man
hung a
shingle

outside
his house

that said

lessons

in how
to be
japan
ese

he taught
his students
to arrange
flowers

to pour
tea

to speak
japanese,
of course,

to write
haiku

to open
fans

to close
parasols

& to
walk
a tight
wire

this is
all eas
ier for
you than

it is
for us,

said one
of the
students,

being
japanese
yourself

actually,
i'm not
said the
man

i'm a
swede

but my
teacher

was jap
anese

[1970]

the brand new city

A man
had a
plan
for a
brand
new
city

instead
of a
shopping
center

there'd
be a
concert
hall

instead
of a
parking
lot

there'd
be a
museum

instead
of
filling-
stations

there'd
be a
fountain

instead
of
miles
of
white
concrete

there'd
be lots
of trees

the man
was
pleased
with
his
plan

&
so he
presented
it

to the
committee

the
committee
was tired
that year
& said:
we'll
adopt
it

& so
they
built it:

a brand
new
city

way out
on the
plains

of kansas

when
the people
came out
to live
in it

they
said

that it
didn't
have
any
of
the
things
they
were
used
to

& that
it was
all
full
of
things

that
they
didn't
know
how
to
use

&
they
won
dered
what
they
were
going
to
do

we'll
live
in it,

said
one
man

&
build
a
shop
ping
center

we'll
live
in it,
said
another

&
build
a
parking
lot

we'll
live
in it

said
a third

&
make
con
crete
walks

when
the man
heard
what
they
had
done

he said
it wasn't
too bad

& again

that it
was
better

than
nothing

[1970]

sun poems

1973

trans
lu
cent

stone

trans
lu
cent

hill

trans
lu
cent

sky

trans
lu
cent

tree

-

trans
lu
cent

rocks

trans
lu
cent

sea

trans
lu
cent

sky

trans
lu
cent

tree

-

a

sun

a

sun

at

the

cen

ter

of

the

earth

a

sun

a

sun

at

the

cen

ter

of

the

sky

at
the
cen
ter
of
the
earth

a
blaz
ing
bright
ness

a
black
black
spot

at
the
cen
ter

of
the
sky

-

at
the
cen
ter
of
the
earth

a
blaz
ing
sea

at
the
cen
ter
of
the
sky

a
whirl
ing
hill

a
blaz
ing
sea

a
blaz
ing
sea

a
whirl
ing
rock

a
whirl
ing
hill

-

at
the
cen
ter
of
the
earth

a
seed
of
flame

at
the
cen
ter
of
the
sun

a
leaf
of
ash

at
the
cen
ter
of
the
earth

a
seed
of
flame

at
the
cen
ter
of
the
sun

an
ash

-

the
fire

the
fire

at
the
cen
ter
of
the
earth

the
sun

the
sun

at
the
cen
ter
of
the
sky

the
fire

the
fire

at
the
cen
ter
of
the
earth

the
sun

at
the
cen
ter
of
the
sky

-

four poems

I
am
the
way
I
am

you
are
the
way
you
are

I
am
the
way
I
am

you
are
the
way

you
are

I
made
my
self
the
way
I
am

you
made
your
self
the
way
you
are

you
made
me

as
I
am

I
made
you
as
you
are

you
made
me
as
I
am

I
made
you
as
you
are

I
made
my
self
the
way
I
am

I
made
my
self

you
made
your
self

I
made
my
self

you	the	the	the
made	way	way	way
your	I	you	you
self	am	are	are)

I	you	(you	-
made	made	made	
my	your	your	
self	self	self	

[1972]

I   I
am   am
lost   found

I   I
am   am
lost   found

I   you
am   are
found   lost

I   you
am   are
found   lost

I
am   you
lost   are
             found
I
am   you
lost   are
             found

you   I
are   am
found   lost

you
are   -
found

[1972]

Maude	Maude	Maude
my	my	my
dear	dear	dear
we	Charles	Charles
have	my	my
reached	dear	dear
the		
end	this	this
of	is	is
the	the	the
line	end	end
Charles		the
my	this	end
dear	is	
	the	the
we	end	the
have		end
reached		
		-
the		
end		
of		
the		
line		

[1972]

(a re   con
prise)   clu
                   sions

the
song
is   I
o   made
ver   my
                   self

this
is   the
its   way
con   I
clu   am
sion

                   you
the   made
song   your
is   self
end
ed   the
                   way
these   you
are   are
its

I	you
made	made
my	your
self	self
the	the
way	way
I	you
am	are

-

[1972]

sea & sky

1965

i.

they
groan

why
do
they
groan

the
people
groan

why
do
the
people
groan

the
nations
groan

why
do
the
nations
groan

?

why
do
the
nations
groan

&
why

do
they
re-
peat

a
vain
thing

?

the
clouds

the
clouds

are
ris-
ing

(over
the
sea)

the winter

the winter

(is
com-
ing)

sit
closer

to-
geth-
er

sit
closer

as
well

to
the
earth

(for
the
cold

comes
on)

the
earth

the
earth

in
all

its
seasons

in
all

its
seasons

in
all

its
seasons

the
earth

the
earth

the
earth

not

thus
&
thus

&
thus

&
thus

but
thus

&
thus

&
thus

not
thus
&
thus

&

thus

&

thus

but

thus

&

thus

&

thus

a
cer-
tain

rhythm

a
cer-
tain

know-
ing

to
be

ob-
serv-
'd

to
be
re-
mark-
'd

a
cer-
tain

rhythm

a
cer-
tain

know-
ing

(in
all

the
chang-
ing

days)

prais-
ing

this
mo-
ment

with
all
of
his

heart

gave
him
heart

gave
him

heart

for
the

next

prais-
ing
this
mo-
ment

with
all
of
his

heart

gave
him
heart

gave
him

heart

for
what

fol-
low-
'd

prais-
ing

this
mo-
ment

with
all
of
his

heart

gave
him
heart

gave
him

heart

for
what

fol-
low-
'd

prais-
ing
this

mo-
ment

with
all

of
his
heart

gave
him
heart

gave
him

heart

for
what

fol-
low-
'd

the
light

the
light

the
eye

the
eye

the
eye

the
eye

the
light

the
light

the
light

the
light

the
eye

the
eye

the
eye

the
eye

the
light

the
light

the
sun

the
sun

the
city

the
city

the
city

the
city

the
sun

the
sun

no
more

the
sun

no
more

the
sun

the
city

the
city

no
more

no
more

no
more

the
sun

no
more

the
city

(no
more)

the
city

the
city

the
city

the
city

the
sun

the
sun

the
sun

the
city

the
city

the
city

the
city

(the
city

the
city)

the
sun

the
city

the
city

(a
sun-
less

cit-
y)

the
city

the
city

(the
sun)

the
city

the
city

(a
sun-
less

cit-
y)

the
city

the
city

(the
sun)

why
do
the

na-
tions

groan

why
do
the

na-
tions

trem-
ble

why
do
the

na-
tions

groan

&
trem-
ble

(&
the
peo-
ple

re-
peat

a
vain

thing)

?

ii.

the
world

the
world

with-
in

with-
in

the
world

the
world

with-
in

with-
in

the
world

the
world

with-
in

with-
in

that
sings

that
sings

that
sings

salt

salt

sweet

salt

no

tear

of

cloud

no

tear

con-

tains

sea's

wis-

dom

salt

sweet

salt

salt

salt

sweet

salt

no

tear

of

cloud

no

tear

con-

tains

sea's

wis-

dom

salt

sweet

salt

the
fire

the
fire

of
thorn

of
thorn

the
fire

the
fire

of
thorn

of
thorn

of

thorn

of

thorn

a

fire

a

fire

a

fire

a

fire

of

thorn

the
dove

the
dove

the
dove

the
dove

comes
down

comes
down

&
breaks
the
air

the
dove

the
dove

the
dove

the
dove

comes
down

&
breaks

the
air

look
look

what
circles

these

now
whis-
per

whis-
per

through

the
sea

look
look

what
circles

these

now
whis-
per

(end-
less)

through

the
seas

the

words

the

words

of

heav-

'n

re-

fin-

'd

the

words

the

words

of

heav-

'n

re-

fin-

'd

the

words

the

words

of

heav-

'n

re-

fin-

'd

re-

fin-

'd

re-

fin-

'd

re-

fin-

'd

all

a-

like

&

all

the

same

all

a-

like

&

all

the

same

no-

thing

no-

thing

no-
thing

chang-
es

no-
thing

no-
thing

no-
thing

new

iii.

              black
              the
              warp

              &
              red
              the
              woof

              black
              the
              warp

              &
              red
              the
              woof

              red
              the
              woof

&
black
the
warp

red
the
woof

&
black
the
warp

black
the
warp

&
red
the
woof

black
the
warp

&
red
the
woof

tight
tight

the
string

of
the
harp

he
was
play-
ing

tight
tight

the
song

he
had
learn-
'd

to
in-
dite

tight
tight

the
string

of
the
harp

he
was
play-
ing

tight
tight

the
song

he
had
made

his
bas-
ket

his
bas-
ket

was
wov-
en

of
words

his
bas-
ket

his
bas-
ket

was
wov-
en

of
words

his
words

were
wove
tight

as
a
bas-
ket

a
bas-
ket

his
bas-
ket

his
bas-
ket

was
wov-
en

of
words

what
was
the
song

that
his
heart

was
in-
dit-
ing

what
was
the
song

that
his
heart

was
in-
dit-
ing

?

his

heart

was

in-

dit-

ing

the

song

of

his

love

his

heart

was

in-

dit-

ing

his

love

what
was
the
love

that
his
heart

was
in-
dit-
ing

?

a
love

a
love

a
mys-
ter-
i-
ous

love

what
was
the
love

that
his
heart

was
in-
dit-
ing

?

a
love

a
mys-
ter-
i-
ous

love

black
black

the
warp

tight
tight

the
string

red
red

the
woof

of
my
love

of
my
love

black
black

the
warp

tight
tight

the
string

red
red

the
woof

of
my
love

a
sweet
wind

a
sweet
wind

blows
from
the

south

(but
my
love

is
far

a-
way)

a
sweet
wind

a
sweet
wind

blows
from
the

south

(but
my
heart

sings

wel-
a-
day)

iv.

all
dreams

one
dream

all
mes-
sage

one
mes-
sage

all
mes-
sage

one
mes-
sage

all
dreams

one
dream

all
dreams

all
dreams

one
dream

one
dream

all
dreams

all
dreams

one
dream

one
dream

the

seas

the

seas

the

sea

the

sea

the

seas

the

seas

the

sea

the

sea

sea-
sons

&

sea-
sons

sea-
sons

&

sea-
sons

the
seas

the
seas

the
sea

all
dreams

one
dream

all
dreams

one
dream

the
sea-
sons

the
sea-
sons

the
sea

the
sea

the
sea

the
sea

the
sea

the
sea

the
sea

(the

sea

in
its

sea-
sons)

(the
sea

in
its

sea-
sons)

the
sea

the
sea

the
sea

the
sun

the
sun

the
sea

the
sun

the
sun

the
sea

(the
sea

in

its

sea-
sons)

(the

sun

in

its

sea-

sons)

the

sea

the

sea

the

sea

these

are

the

sea-

sons

of

sun

&

sea

these

are

the

sea-

sons

of

sun

&

sea

the
sun

the
sun

the
sea

the
sea

the
sun

the
sun

the
sea

the
sea

the
sun

the
sun

the
sea

the
sea

the
sun

the
sun

the
sea

the
sea

that

ev-

'ry

span-

gle

dap-

pl-

'd

ban-

gle

sing

sing

sing

sing

that

ev-

'ry

span-
gle

dap-
pl-
'd

ban-
gle

sing

sing

sing

the
sun

the
sun

is
on

the

sea

the
sun

the
sun

is
on

the
sea

the
sun

the
sun

is
on

the
sea

the
sun

is
on

the
sea

that

ev-

'ry

span-

gle

dap-

pl-

'd

ban-

gle

sing

sing

sing

sing

that

ev-

'ry

span-
gle

dap-
pl-
'd

ban-
gle

sing

sing

sing

the
word

the
word

is

a

fly-
ing
bird

(a
bird

a
bird

a
bird)

the
word

the
word

is

a

fly-
ing

bird:

a
bird

a
bird

a
bird

v.

steer

your

course

steer

your

course

by

this

wheel

by

this

wheel

steer

your

course

steer

your

course

by
this

wheel

by
this

wheel

by
this

wheel

by
this

wheel

steer
your
course

steer
your
course

by
this

wheel

by
this

wheel

steer
your

course

the
sea

the
sea

(the
bos-
om

of
the
sea)

the
sea

the
sea

(the
bos-
om

of

the
sea)

bos-
om

bos-
om

(the
bos-
om

of
the
sea)

the
sea

the
sea

(the
bos-
om

of
the
sea)

the
sea

the
sea

(the
bos-
om

of
the

sea)

bos-
om

bos-
om

(the
bos-
om

of
the
sea)

bos-
om

bos-
om

(the
bos-
om

of
the

sea)

if
i
were

a
bird

i
would
fly

i
would
fly

out
ov-
er

the
sea

out
ov-
er

the
sea

if
i
were

a
bird

i
would
fly

i
would
fly

out
ov-
er

the
sea

out
ov-
er

the
sea

out
ov-
er

the
sea

i
would
fly

i
would
fly

i
would

fly

out
ov-
er
the
sea

out
ov-
er

the
sea

i
would
fly

i
would
fly

i
would

fly

the

far-

off

cit-

y

the

far-

off

cit-

y

light

the

light

on

the

far-

off

cit-

y

the
far-
off

cit-
y

the
far-
off

cit-
y

the
light

the
light

the
light

if
i
were

a
bird

if
i
were

a
bird

i
would
fly

i
would
fly

(to
the
far-
off

cit-
y)

if
i
were

a
bird

if
i
were

a
bird

i
would
fly

i
would
fly

i
would
fly

out
ov-
er

the
sea

out
ov-
er

the
sea

i
would
fly

i
would

fly

i
would

fly

out

ov-

er

the

sea

out

ov-

er

the

sea

i

would

fly

i

would

fly

i
would

fly

the
light

the
light

is
on

the
sea

the
light

is
on

the
sea

the
light

the
light

is
on

the
sea

the
light

is
on

the

sea

the
cit-
y

the
cit-
y

the
far-
off

cit-
y

(the
light

is
on

the
sea)

the
cit-
y

the
cit-
y

the
far-
off

cit-
y

(the
light

is
on

the

sea)

the
light

the
light

the
sea

the
sea

(the
light

the
light

the
sea

the
sea)

vi.

the
slow-
est

the
slow-
est

of
move-
ments

of
move-
ments

a-
long

the
sur-
face

of
the

sea

the
slow-
est

the
slow-
est

of
move-
ments

of
move-
ments

a-
long

the
sur-
face

of
the

sea

be-
cause

the
changes

be-
cause

the
changes

of
sea

are
the
changes

of
mu-
sic

be-
cause

the
changes

be-
cause

the
changes

of
sea

are
the

changes

of
mu-
sic

the
slow-
est

of
move-
ments

the
slow-
est

of
move-
ments

is
on

the
sea

is
on

the
sea

as

oce-

an

as

oce-

an

re-

flects

the

sky

the

cities

of

man

the

cit-

y

(of

God)

as

oce-

an

as

oce-

an

re-

flects

the

sky

the

cit-

ies

of

man

(of

God)

what
cur-
rent

what
cur-
rent

is
un-
der

the
sea

what
cur-
rent

what
cur-
rent

is
un-
der

the
sea

cold
cur-
rent

warm
cur-
rent

smooth
cur-
rent

strong
cur-
rent

(cur-
rent)

what
cur-
rent

is
un-
der

the
sea

?

the
sun
smiles

the
sea
smiles

the
moon
smiles

the
sea
smiles

light

light

on
the
sea

(on
the
sea)

light

light

(on
the
sea)

the
sky

is
one

the
air

is
one

the
sea

the
sea

the
sea

is
one

the

sky

is

one

the

air

is

one

the

sea

the

sea

the

sea

the
sea

may
reach

the
sea

may

reach

but
on-
ly
the
sky

but
on-
ly

the
sky

the
sea

may
reach

the
sea

may

reach

but
on-
ly

the
sky

(leans
down)

the
sea

may

reach

the
sea

may

reach

but
on-
ly

the
sky

but
on-
ly

the
sky

the
sea

may
reach

the
sea

may

reach

but
on-
ly

the
sky

(leans
down)

the
dark-
ness

the
dark-
ness

(the
face

of

the

sea)

the
dark-
ness

the
dark-
ness

(the
face

of

the

sea)

vii.

                    how
                    still

                    how
                    still

                    (&
                    the
                    domes

                    how
                    still)

                    how
                    still

                    how
                    still

                    is
                    the

                    sea

how
still

how
still

(&
the
domes
how
still)

how
still

the
wind-
less

sea

the
sea

the
sea

the
air

the
air

the
sky

the
sky

the
sky

the
sea

the
sea

the
air

the
air

the
sky

the
sky

the
sky

the

air

is

a

gi-

ant

who

holds

his

hand

be-

tween

the

sea

&

the

sky

the

air

is

a

gi-
ant:

he
holds

his
hand

be-
tween

the
sea

&

the
sky

the
dream-
ing

dream-
ing

sea

re-
gards

the

smil-
ing

sky

the
dream-
ing

dream-
ing

sea

re-
gards

the
smil-
ing

sky

the
dream-
ing

sea

the
smil-
ing

sky

the
dream-
ing

dream-
ing

sea

the

dream-

ing

sea

the

smil-

ing

sky

the

dream-

ing

dream-

ing

sea

(the

sea

may

reach

the
sea

may
reach)

the
sky

looks
down

looks

down

(the
sea

may
reach

the
sea

may

reach)

the
sky

looks
down

looks

down

if
i

were
a
bird

if
i

were
a
bird

i
would

fly

to
the
ends

of
the

sea

if

i

were

a

bird

if

i

were

a

bird

i

would

fly

to

the

ends

of

the

sea

the
sea

the
sea

the
sky

the
sky

the
sky

the
sky

the
sea

the
sea

the
sea

the
sea

the
sky

the
sky

the
sky

the
sky

the
sea

the
sea

the
domes

the
domes

are
still

are
still

the
sea

the
sea

is
still

the
domes

are
still

the
sea

is

still

the
air

is
still

is
still

(the
domes

are
still

the
sea

is
still)

the
air

is

still

is

still

what
are

the
cur-
rents

un-
der

the
sea

what
are

the
cur-
rents

un-
der

the
sea

(the
sea

is

a

dream-

ing

sea)

what

are

the

cur-

rents

un-

der

the

sea

what

are

the

cur-

rents

un-

der

the

sea

(the
sea-
's

a
yearn-
ing

sea)

the
sea

may
reach

the
sea

may

reach

(the
sky

looks
down

looks

down)

the
sea

may
reach

the
sea

may

reach

(the
sky

looks
down

looks

down)

what

are

the

cur-

rents

un-

der

the

sea

(the

sea

is

a

dream-

ing

sea)

what

are

the

cur-

rents

un-

der

the

sea

(the

sea-

's

a

yearn-

ing

sea)

the
air

the
air

the
sky

the
sky

the
sea

the
sea

the
sea

the
air

the
air

the
sky

the
sky

the
sea

the
sea

the
sea

acknowledgments

This project would not have happened without the vision of Joshua Beckman, who has been a terrifically insightful partner in planning the book. Robert Lax was long blessed with publishers who understood his work at the deepest intuitive level, and Joshua fits perfectly in that line. & many thanks to everyone else at Wave: Heidi Broadhead, Alexander Moysaenko, Rachel Welty, Brittany Dennison, Matthew Zapruder, Charlie Wright. I was introduced to the work of Robert Lax many years ago when Connie Brothers stopped me in a hallway to ask if I wanted to spend part of a summer in Greece; ever since, she and Marcia Kelly, Robert Lax's nieces, have been like a second family, and their enthusiasm and generous encouragement were invaluable. Paul Spaeth, director of the Friedsam Memorial Library, at St. Bonaventure University, was an impeccable host and sounding board during research trips. Many thanks are due as well to the staff at Columbia University's Rare Book & Manuscript Library. I visited Columbia in part due to the advice of my Portland State colleague Michael McGregor, whose biography of Lax promises to give the poetry the careful contextualization it has long deserved. My research was also aided by the detailed Lax bibliography prepared by Sigrid Hauff. In preparing my own introduction, I drew upon *Merton & Friends*, a triple biography of Thomas Merton, Lax, and Ed Rice, by James Harford, as well as David Miller and Rupert Loydell's encyclopedic collection *The ABCs of Robert Lax*. & through all these efforts, sometimes in the same room, sometimes a continent away, Judith Goldman was my constant companion.